I0470572

How We Raised Over 245% of Our Goal With Our FIRST Crowd-Funding Project!

And hit the goal in 21 hours!

Carl E. Jones, CFP ®

a.k.a. Topper The Magic Clown

With Marsha Jones, a.k.a. Twinkle!

CARL E. JONES, CFP ®

Copyright © 2013 Carl E. Jones, CFP ®

All rights reserved.

ISBN: 1492263427
ISBN-13: 978-1492263425

DEDICATION

It's hard to write this with Twinkle's help and
keep this dedication a secret from her!

She believed in me and in our project from the beginning.
She let me have free reign to follow my heart and my vision
for this. And she was a great cheerleader along the way too!

This wouldn't have happened without her and without her
I wouldn't have had the heart to do it. She's the best!
All my love to you Twinkle!
Carl

CARL E. JONES, CFP ®

CONTENTS

CHAPTER 1 - WHY?

Why have a crowd-funding project in the first place? It can't be just about the money. *It's "GOTTA" be about more than that,* in my opinion.

Maybe I should say that OUR project was more – a LOT more – than that. And since this book is, after all, about our project, I'll try to keep from climbing up on the soapbox and preaching about how YOUR project should be done. Fair enough?

So let's start over, shall we?

Why have a crowd-funding project in the first place? That's for YOU to decide, not me to dictate. However, there are a few thoughts along those lines I'd like share with you, please.

When you do some research on your potential topic *(you HAVE already researched it, right?)* you'll find that you might be 1 of 100 projects actively seeking funds along the same lines as your project. Or, as I found out, you might be one of virtually NO other projects actively seeking funding along the same lines. Which is best? Who cares? You can't control it. **Do NOT get bogged down in minutia which you can't control. Move on.**

Decide what the project is to really be about. A product? A charity? A need for you or a group or a school, etc… Basically, <u>**you have to have a goal.**</u> You have to know where you are going before you get in the car! Old advice but still 100% appropriate.

However, I suspect if you are reading this you already have an idea in mind so let's move past this point and get down to where the proverbial rubber meets the road, shall we? That's another oldie but goodie, we said thousands of to many times when I was spending my youth playing C&W records at a radio station.

If **you** like the idea, the entire point of a CFC (Crowd Funding Campaign) is to find other like-minded souls who not only agree with you but *will help you take it from just a nebulous dream into reality.* They can participate, albeit usually minimally, but they CAN participate and say they helped the XYZ Widget become reality. Some of the widgets out there are AMAZING!! And it's only going to get bigger and cooler and more amazing!

Some CFC's aren't about widgets. They are to help people, help groups, fund research, go across the country, etc… All are ideas, but not all will find willing participants who will fork over funds to make it come true. And thus the nature of CFC's.

So as you think of YOUR CFC, ask yourself what the likelihood is that it will be successful. Write that down. Fold it up. Put it in an envelope **and then shred it** That's what I said. Shred, toss, grind, rip, burn, etc.. because NOBODY has a true clue what will work and to what degree. In many ways, it's like going to Vegas. Fun – but who knows what will happen. The difference is that what happens in Vegas MIGHT stay in Vegas, but what happens on the CFC front, is pretty much public forever. The clarity and the transparency are part of the machine that gives us some confidence that we aren't being taken to the cleaners.

By the way, on that topic ---- READ WHAT EACH CFC website says. I think you'll discover that once you give your money, there is nothing you can do if the project's creator doesn't fulfill their end of the deal. Read and research that for yourself but that's what I've found in the various websites I investigated prior to launching my CFC on Indiegogo. As a project creator with a strong sense of doing what is right as part of my upbringing, (not to mention the number of family members, clients, prospective clients, church members, fellow entertainers, medical personnel that actually treat me and neighbors that helped fund it – plus the CFP Board always there with open eyes) the LAST thing on this earth that would happen on my project is that I wouldn't honor everything I said I would do on it. But not everybody is honest. Buyer/donor/project coordinator beware.

If you will research a wide variety of projects on a wide variety of CFC websites (just Google them, there are a

LOT) you'll see projects that didn't get a PENNY but you'll think they are incredibly wonderful. And other CFC that look like the worst, most stupid waste of money on earth, OVERFUNDED by tens of thousands of dollars. Truly amazing and confusing all at the same time to me. And that, my friends, is the pond into which you are about to go swimming.

1. Do your research!

2. Do MORE research!

3. Know inside and out what other similar projects asked for, and got.

4. Know ALL of the perks the other similar projects offered.

5. Pick the best of the best of the other perks, and make yours better.

6. Try to have a project that you are passionate about.

7. Ignore suggestion #6.

8. ONLY DO THIS if you ARE passionate about the project.

9. Do more research.

10. Get some help. You CANNOT do this alone!

CHAPTER 2 - RESEARCH

You noticed at the end of Chapter 1, I overemphasized doing research. Let me say it again. ***DO MORE RESEARCH! Then, once your mind is made up, go with your decision and don't look back.*** Right or wrong, YOU, the project LEADER, have got to **L E A D!** That means no more wishy-washy chit-chat. It means you ARE moving forward and you WILL do what it takes to be successful. PERIOD!

What kind of research, you might be casually asking yourself. I think it falls into 3 main categories.

First – what does your family think of the project. While you're at it, ask your close friends too. Especially ask the ones who tell you the truth.

Second – the research that I conducted included quite a few other CFC sites where I looked for similar projects. Finding VERY few gave me raw data to toss into the blender for consideration.

Third – the internet. See if your new widget idea is already out there. See what you can find. Document what you find. Print and save it. KNOW YOUR SUBJECT MATERIAL VERY WELL!

Once you have all of that research done, have a few close friends Google the topic of your CFC and see what they come up with. You more than likely WILL be surprised.

Once you have the research done and reviewed and summarized, then you can move forward. Remember, this is YOUR baby. Does the research suggest it will be successful or that it won't make the cut? YOU have to see how the CFC project looks in light of all this great info you are now swimming in.

Not every idea is a good idea for a CFC. YOU have to decide if yours is a good idea, or not. If it is, GREAT! Keep reading. If it's not, then no big deal! Toss it and come up with a better idea or a different angle. ONE "NO" does NOT a disaster make!

After you've done the research and you are confident that you know your subject VERY well, start putting down in your computer or a notebook, the different main points you feel are important. Then, under each of them, list things that go with them from your research. You may want to refer to those points as you prepare your video or your site. Remember, you did the research, **now USE IT to your advantage!** If experts say things that support your idea, it's a good idea to share that with others.

I don't want you to get bogged down in the research because you run the risk of "paralyzation by analyzation" and that is never productive. But you must find the balance between getting ready and actually doing the project! You have to know more than enough, but you don't have to have a graduate degree from Princeton University to do a project.

Now you also need to remember this – *You only get one chance to make a good first impression!* If you "blow it" when people go to your site and read your material or watch your video, you can color them gone…

Know what you are talking about and then

DO IT!

Let nothing stand in your way!

CHAPTER 3 - DOING IT!

Let's start where we left off in Chapter 2. DO IT! It's time to get busy or go home!

You have a good idea. You have SOLID research. You have a PLAN! Right?   *__NO?!?__*   **Rut-ro**……..

Okay, it's time to make a plan!

First things first – get a cup of coffee. Extra caffeine! Why? Not just because I really love coffee, but because the extra caffeine will help you! Remember --- ***__ENTHUSIASM SELLS!!__*** *If you are not personally ENTHUSIASTIC about this project, then drop the idea right now… It's going to die on the vine if you don't.*

Why would Joe Schmo in Tim-Buck-Too, Iowa get excited about your project if YOU aren't excited? The answer is – he won't!

Jump up and down. Run around the desk. Drink more coffee. Do SOMETHING to get that enthusiasm ramped up.

Good – I feel it emanating from you right now! Yee-Haa! Let's go!

So what IS your plan? It's not all fun and games, kiddos! Let's look at things that should be on your plan, shall we?

1. How are you going to get the word out to the world?

2. How OFTEN are you going to get the word out there?

3. What about a video?

*   **DO NOT DO THIS WITHOUT A VIDEO!!***

4. What about letters of reference to put on the site?

5. What kind of pictures can/should you use?

6. What perks/rewards will you offer?

7. Are the perks enough or are they TOOOO MUCH?

8. Who is your Executive GOTTA Have 'Em Assistant?

9. What day of the week will you start?

10. How long is your funding period?

11. Do you take whatever you get or only if you get it all?

12. Do you have a PayPal & bank account set up?

13. How much are you going to try and raise?

14. What do you feel will be the range of donations?

15. What will you do if you don't raise enough money?

And those are just the starting questions. Each of them have questions behind them. Work on those for a few minutes while I go get another cup of coffee….

Okay --- let's not panic. Yes, that is a long list. But some are easy!! And you can always select the "default" option (what I did) and see what happens. Of course, **YOU are the Leader of YOUR project, not me.** So you might want to take some time to think about those in light of what I'm about to say. **It's YOUR project. It's YOUR choice!**

So let's take a bite out of this elephant and get going!! Remember, "there is no time like tomorrow" to do what needs to be done TODAY!

1. *How are you going to get the word out to the world?*

This is worth the price of this book, if you ask me. First, if you aren't on Facebook, Twitter, Linked-In, Pinterest, and MORE, -- *get on them NOW!!!* **You need a WIDE audience on ALL of them! GET BUSY!!!**

Also, get an app like HOOT-SUITE that lets you update your social media homes at one time. My favorite was hoot-suite. I could update both of my FaceBook accounts, Linked-In & Twitter with ONE posting. Sure, it was limited to the length that Twitter would take, but it worked!

There may be other apps or ways that are better. Do some research! New apps come out each day!

I did NOT like the fact that Hoot-Suite wouldn't update Pinterest for me. I had to do that one by myself.

Also, get the app called GLYDER. It's GREAT! It lets you make some good looking "posters" to use to update your social media, email lists, etc… Seriously – it's terrific!!

You aren't the only one that is online! If you have a spouse, or kids, or siblings, or family-in-law, see which (ALL!) of them will regularly post updates to their lists. Trust me, they won't think of this on their own. Nor will they post as many updates as you will. But --- **they WILL post some and some = potential for more!**

You need a LIST of who those folks are. Write it down! The more, the merrier.

Don't forget that you are probably in groups too! You have a lot of contacts that you can update that way as well. Church, business, etc... The more, the _ _ _ _ _ _ _!!

And how do you get a TOTAL STRANGER to put it on their social media page? I made a flier that I carried in the car! I'd pass them out to EVERYBODY! I told them, "I'm not hitting you up for money! I am only asking that you look at the site, watch the video and IF YOU AGREE WITH THE IDEA, share the info on your social media sites. Copies are 10 cents or less. Isn't it worth investing one thin dime to put your message in the hands of someone who has the potential to expose you to

THOUSANDS of others who are NOT already on your list? <u>Sure it is!!</u>

Remember this – if you are spending money with a company, such as a Dry Cleaner, you KNOW they "owe" you, right? ***They should --- at the least --- post your flier, check out your site, and spread the word.*** Plus, of course, make, at the least, a small donation. Why? You spend money with them ALL the time! That's why!

Gas stations, banks, dry cleaners, RESTUARANTS, and more… They are staffed by people who may very well LOVE your idea. Tell them about it! **<u>You can't pass out too many fliers. It's "old school" and it works!</u>**

I didn't get this done and I regret it…. Put a flier on the door of your neighbors. I don't mean 10,000 neighbors. I mean the 5-10 right around you. Do this AND email them!

I didn't do this either and I regret it even more --- ***get a magnetic sign for your car.*** SHORT & SIMPLE! Something like:

Help Me Help Sick Kids

www.topper.us

Sure it's going to cost you a few bucks. Quit whining. Just do it. **You'll thank me.** Of course, that is the message that I would have used. I think you realize you need your own message, right? Speaking of those magnetic car signs, a fun place to eat is FUZZY TACO's. If you have one near one check and see if that location will let you put up a magnetic sign of yours on their walls. The Fuzzy's in this area allow that and it's part of the ambiance. A GREAT idea!

So that is a start. **A START, only!** Keep looking during the life of your project! You might see something that blows all of these out of the water.

2. How OFTEN are you going to get the word out there?

Well, let's just say that there is NO correct answer. One time a day is way too much for some folks and one time a week is way too much for others. YOU have to decide. In my case, I referred to my email updates as a **"tsunami of**

updates". I was SO far over the top that **even I told myself to slow down!** Seriously – I sent a LOT. And then I sent more on top of that...... And our results speak for themselves.....

You have to decide. I believe in "more is better" and some people *HATE* that. Others, like me, **love it.** You decide. It's your project. My advice? Err on the side of overboard..

Short updates are better than long ones. And with your own tsunami of updates, short will work.

3. What about a video?

DO NOT DO THIS
WITHOUT A VIDEO!!
Need I say more? YES!! Do a video!!

Don't waste your time on a project if you don't do a video!

I got lucky! I had a superb videographer and a terrific wife and close friend who all worked with me on the video. It's what it is because of them, NOT because of me! Our videographer gave me a price break since this was to help kids. That helped a lot! But regardless, you must have a good video! It MUST "tell your story." It IS your story!

Be honest. Be natural. Be yourself!

Did I mention, BE YOURSELF? You must let people see the real you and not a fake persona. They are going to give you money – hopefully. They won't do that if they don't believe in you or your project. You can't fake honesty, in my opinion, for very long before it all comes out. Tell the truth and explain EVERYTHING about your project in that video. You want their help??? They want YOUR help to understand WHY they want to pull out their credit card and help you.

I think our video was too long. But we cut and cut and cut and it was as short as I would sign off on. You decide how long your story should take to tell. You are the LEADER, so LEAD! There is NO perfect answer, I assure you.

And once you get that video done, tell the world!! You absolutely MUST HAVE distribution of your message! It's critical to your success.

4. What about letters of reference to put on the site?

By all means get some and get them on the site! These need to be from people who will vouch for you if they are contacted. They need to be people who are commenting on the kind of thing you are doing in the project. For example, don't have someone write a reference letter for you about how good you can sing in church if the project is about raising money to paint an orphanage. This is VERY important. Don't overlook this item.

5. What kind of pictures can/should you use?

I think a lot of pictures help! It depends on your individual project but get as many as are appropriate and put them all over your site.

6. What perks/rewards will you offer?

These need to be appropriate. What do other sites offer? What can you get donated? What does your site ALLOW? Some fundraising sites are VERY specific! Read the info on your site and see what other similar projects are offering and then, make yours BETTER! You need to make it CLEAR on the site what they get. It needs to be very simple and easy to understand. The better the perk, in many cases, the better and bigger the donation.

In our case, about 40% of the donors didn't even request a perk. They just wanted the money used for the kids. That was a wonderful thing for them to do and we are very grateful. But you can NOT count on that! You MUST price your perks so that if everybody requests one, you can get them to them.

As I write this book, we are just about to send out our perks. We've waited, as suggested, until we get the funding but we want to be ready to drop them the day we get the funds. Remember, you are THANKING the folks who helped you. Please don't drop that ball!

We had a LOT of perks that went unclaimed. I was shocked on some of them too. We had others that FLEW out the door. That was great, but surprising. We had others that had to have their donation levels reduced to be selected. Not surprising I suppose.

I gave some perks 4-5 days to generate some interest or I'd pull them, or revamp them. Each time I made ANY changes I sent a notice to EVERYONE. It's important to let folks know because they might have wanted your perk of an XYZ but didn't have $250. They might, however, have $150! Don't think a perk is dead just because it's not picked at first. The price might be to high.

We offered some "thank you certificates" available via download only. We offered some LIGHT WEIGHT perks too for lower donations. All to help save on postage! Keep that in mind!

We had some great perks donated by generous friends. They helped a GREAT deal! If I were doing this same project again, I'd round up some GREAT perks, donated by friends and businesses, to help us. I know a LOT of people do that, but this is your baby we're talking about. Go get some for YOUR project!

<u>We also had perks available ONLY on Day One!</u> That helped! We had some that popped up at odd times during the campaign too. You have to keep the excitement level UP and that's one way of doing it.

7. Are the perks enough or are they TOOOO MUCH?

Common sense should dictate here. Don't offer a new car for a $100 donation. Also, please don't offer only a thank you for a $1,000 donation. What's right for your project? I don't know. You are the leader. It's your call. Be careful and be realistic. Ask for advice from your family and closest friends. You do NOT want to mess this up!

8. Who is your Executive GOTTA Have 'Em Assistant?

You better have a helper regardless of the size of the

project! I was LUCKY that our dear friend Kathi Fowler pitched in to help us, free of charge! She just took the ball and ran with it. There were a LOT of details that she took care of once the project started that would have kept me up all night. Do NOT try to go it alone and NO, Kathi is not "for hire."

Don't let a short paragraph make you think this isn't ULTIMATELY important. It IS that important! I promise!!

9. What day of the week will you start?

Some people might not think this matters. I do and so did my team. We had long talks about this and came to the conclusion that, for us Tuesday at 10am was the best time. Our reasoning was that Tuesday was best since we could reach our audience on Monday to get them ready. We wanted day #1 to be a great day. For us, it was. We hit 100% of our goal in 21 HOURS on a 21 day project.

There are many pros and cons for each day, undoubtedly. I believe you need to pick the day that YOU feel is best for

YOUR project based on your own reasons. However, for my projects, I'm convinced that Tuesday is the best start date.

10. How long is your funding period?

The various platforms have many options. You can run some projects up to 60 days. One site says projects of 30 days or less have much better results. Check each site for their updated comments on this.

My belief was that 30 days was to long. Two weeks was too short. So, 21 days got the nod. It let people out of town, or really tied up on other things, have enough time to help us but NOT so much time as for them to think "I'll do this later." I think 3 weeks is plenty of time on most projects. It was for us and honestly, I'm not so sure that 2 weeks wouldn't have been about the same, or better.

My thoughts on this are that the next project will likely be 15 days, or so. Again, it's YOUR project. What do YOU feel is best for YOUR team?

CARL E. JONES, CFP ®

The downside with a short time frame is that you won't be able to reach out to as many people who are NOT on your email or social media lists. If you are going to ACTIVELY work that angle – and you SHOULD – then maybe 3 weeks is the best time frame, if not longer. There is no way to know for certain. You'll have to go with your research, advice and your gut.

11. Do you take whatever you get or only if you get it all?

Some platforms and programs have an option of getting anything you raise, even if you don't hit your goal, and others force the issue and ONLY pay you if you hit your goal. You might be thinking, "why not set a goal of $100, hit it and get that over with?" My thoughts on that are simple. If you are going to 'play games" with the system, what reasonable person will trust you with your project? Not me!

You need to have a reasonable goal that you can justify and you need to explain it in your material. It's not complicated.

On platforms with two options, such as Indiegogo was when we did our project, you have to decide which you want to use. I selected the take anything we raise option. Oddly enough, that wasn't my first choice! However, due to the restrictions they had on acceptable methods of payment based on the anything or all method, I felt I needed to go with the "take anything we get" approach to widen the payment options.

Honestly, I didn't hear ANYTHING from anyone on that issue. I have come to realize that I don't think the average person who will donate to you knows or cares about that issue, at all.

Beyond that however, is the reality that if your project can NOT work without the full amount, then you should ONLY do the method where you only get the money if you get ENOUGH to actually make the project work. Anything else is being dishonest.

12. Do you have a PayPal, bank account & Amazon account?

If you don't have these set up now, stop everything and **GET them set up**. Don't do anything else until this is done. Seriously. ***Stop reading and fix that right now!***

13. How much are you going to try and raise?

You have to decide what's best for you based on honest research, honest projections and an honest assessment of your situation. Is it possible to do it for $1,000? Then why ask for $50,000? If you need $25,000 then why set a goal of $15,000? You need to KNOW YOUR NUMBERS! People will ask and you need to be able to explain your reasoning.

14. What do you feel will be the range of donations?

This isn't a huge issue, in my opinion, but it's important. We expected a LOT of smaller donations. We got 2. Two. Yep, as in 1-2. We averaged about $85 per contribution. That's a much higher range than we thought the average would be. We're happy but a bit surprised.

The issue is that you need to have a good range of perks available based on what you think people will donate. If all of your perks are UNDER the average donation, you'll drive down your average donation. If the perks are higher than your average then you'll scare some folks away. It's a guessing game if it's your first campaign. In most cases, and at least with Indiegogo when we did our project, you could add or delete or change perks, based on their guidelines, through the project. They did have a limit of 20 active perks at one time. You have to have an idea of your donation range since you don't want to use up all of your available perks for a donation range that never happens.

15. What will you do if you don't raise enough money?

If you go for the "full funding or nothing" option, no problem. You raise it or you get nothing. That can be scary. But if you need $10,000 and only raise $2,500 there is no way you can honor your commitment to meet the projects stated objectives. You have to be fair and honest to the people who will donate to you. Tell the truth. Set the goals accurately and work hard to reach them!

CHAPTER 4 - PRE-LAUNCH ACTIVITIES

There are a LOT of things that we did that were a big help. There are a lot of other things we didn't do from the beginning that we added during the campaign. *These are worth the price of this book, if you'll use them.*

First, on paper, list ALL of your social media outlets like FaceBook, Twitter, etc... Next list all of those for your spouse. Then decide if you will update only your accounts or if you can update the accounts of your spouse as well.

Next, make a list of ALL of the businesses you physically visit. They need to get a flyer in their hands at least 3-4 times during the campaign! Put them on a schedule and write down who will take the flier to them & when!

Change the flier a little bit. Print it on colored paper and change the color each time. Do some in a horizontal orientation and others in a vertical orientation.

On the fliers past week #1, be certain to include an update on your stats so they will know that you are WORKING HARD on this and you are being successful!

List all of your friends that you think might even remotely consider putting a flier on the board at their office, church, etc… Mail them 10 fliers each week!

Get your family members on a list too. Hopefully email AND a mailing list. They will hopefully help you. Mail them 10 fliers each week too. It does NOT matter where they live! This is an international world we are looking for help from. We had donations from 4 countries on our campaign. I'll bet you can get 10 without trying!

You need to leave fliers wherever you can. I left some at almost every place I visited. I had them in my hand and sometimes just walked out without them. Silly old memory! What was I thinking???

In my case I HEAVILY, HEAVILY promoted having a HUGE "Day One!" I believed then and now that a BIG Day One will set the tone. In our case we were looking for $4,999 in 21 DAYS. We raised $4,999+ in 21 HOURS. Why? I had a LOT of folks that believed in this project and they wanted to make sure Day One was a HUGE success! They did it, too!! And so can you!

I promoted Day One for at least 3 weeks. I promoted it at least daily and many times MORE than once a day. I felt that made a difference in cutting through the clutter of the billion and a half other things vying for the attention of everybody on the list.

ENTHUSIAM SELLS!

Always has. Always will!

You are the cheerleader. You are the newsman. You are the paperboy screaming *"EXTRA, EXTRA, READ ALL ABOUT IT!!!"* Do your job. ☺

We didn't do this but next time I will! Get some inexpensive business cards, like Vista Print, and put your message on one side and the website & your contact info on the other. Leave them everywhere!!

Books on Guerilla Marketing are everywhere. This is a GREAT chance to use some of those ideas! Experiment and good luck!!

<u>Who is going to benefit from your project? Get THEM on your team and get them INVOLVED!</u>

Once you get the campaign started, **<u>you MUST keep the momentum moving.</u>**

Work harder & longer.

Change the perks. Add some, delete others.

Do whatever you can honestly and ethically do to keep that momentum moving!

CHAPTER 5 - NATIONAL PUBLICITY

We didn't dream of this when we started but we were on the radar screen for 2 national opportunities! While neither worked out, we did light up their screen! That was quite an exciting thing for us!

Five Hour Energy has a "helping hands" project. They saw our project and were impressed. However, they were looking for projects where the leaders had overcome some really tough circumstances to start their project. We didn't fit their needs. No problem.

Also, Fox TV contacted us as they were starting a new show on Crowd Funding. However, we are in the USA and they were not. We lost out on that but again, talk about EXCITING!!

If you wanted to get some local publicity, and you are off to a GREAT start, there is NO reason why you can't try to get the attention of your local media! Google Jeff Crilly's book on how to do that and get it. You'll have a GREAT chance and it will make a BIG difference!

If your project is unique or your way of getting it noticed is unique, they you are 85% of the way there on getting some local publicity. Newsrooms can be BORING much of the time. **They need your help to liven things up!**

Get Jeff's book and you'll see some AMAZING information!

CHAPTER 6 - LAUNCH DAY!

Promote this day/event <u>heavily.</u> <u>Before</u> Launch Day. And MOST CERTAINLY <u>DURING</u> Launch Day!

If you have a great Launch Day you have set the pace of the campaign. If you die on the vine on Day One, it's going to be a long, hard climb out of that hole.

<u>Tell everyone! Tell them again! Find new people & tell them!</u> Email, call, drop by, text, send smoke signals, but get the word OUT!! Then get it out again and again!

Remember those lists you made? Contact them!! One way or the other**<u>, you MUST get the word out to everyone in the universe!!</u>**

CHAPTER 7 - FOCUS ON YOUR DONORS

I really don't think I can emphasize this too much. These are the people who, out of the kindness of their hearts have funded your dream. ***Thank them and thank them again!*** I tried to keep our donors updated VERY frequently both during the campaign and since it ended as part of continually thanking them. **They are THE reason your dream will have legs!!**

Of course getting their perks to them is very important but also letting them know that you appreciate them, other than just one time, is, I believe, really crucial. Their funds are "working" along the way so I believe it's important to thank them along the way too.

This is based on your situation and your style and what your donors prefer but simply put –

THANK THEM OFTEN!!

CHAPTER 8 - UPDATING DONORS & OTHERS

It's clearly important to update everyone. How much to say and how often to say it is an art, not a science. You, your style, your personality and your donors preferences will be a huge part of determining how often to let them know what is going on.

There are some, very few for us, that simply donated to get the perk and they've said "no thanks" to the updates. That is perfectly fine and we are not offended. **<u>You might want to ask them if they want updates.</u>** We did and that's how we found out some didn't want them. In my opinion, this is a really important point that should NOT be overlooked.

You can update some people 1 time a week and it's too much. Others, 1 time a month is too much. Others, 2 times per DAY is not enough. You're going to have to figure out what works for YOU and for your donors.

Also, you need to **keep things fresh!** It is important to remember that old saying, "Out of sight is out of mind!" You don't want your project to fade away. Even after someone donates, they might donate again and **they certainly know other people who can donate.** Our BIGGEST single donation came from a friend of a donor who gave a check to the friend to send to me. They never saw the website or got any information other than what our donor told them. They didn't want a perk. They just wanted to help!

I totally went overboard on updates. I know I did. I don't deny it. However, I've always felt that, for me, it was better to err on the side of too many than too few. That is YOUR call to make on your project.

You do NOT want to give the impression that you have their money and you're gone. Updates will help prevent that from happening. For those who haven't donated yet, an update will keep you fresh in their mind and that is a VERY important thing to do!

It's also important to use your updates as a clock. Let people know that the clock is ticking. Let them know that there is only X amount of time left. Let them know what THEIR generous donation will allow you to do. Tell them. Then, tell them _ _ _ _ _. ☺

As we neared the end of the campaign, I felt like an "on the scene" news reporter. I had updates on all my social media at least 2-3 times an hour and to my email lists about every 2 hours. YES, I did "tick off" some people. I am sorry. But, **I was raising money to help sick kids**. That was more important to me than someone getting temporarily unhappy with me over yet another email. YOU must decide for yourself how you feel about that and how you'll handle it.

<u>Simply put ---</u>

<u>UPDATE</u>

CHAPTER 9 - CAMPAIGN MANAGEMENT

First things first. Get a helper. Got one? No? **Stop reading and find one! Seriously!** I've said it before and I'll say it again **--- *you can't do this on your own. You need a helper*.** We had the best helper in the world! And she knew we needed her before we knew it. She is a long-time friend who knew what to do, and did it. I say this without any exaggeration – without Kathi, we would have been up the proverbial creek without that paddle you hear so much about! If I thanked her every hour, on the hour, for weeks, it wouldn't tell her how much we appreciated her! ***She did a phenomenal job on everything she touched!***

During the campaign, there are a lot of things that fall under the heading of campaign management. Keeping up with the perks, finding new perks, doing updates, making new fliers, passing them out, and on and on and on…. Get a helper!! You will thank me for this, I assure you!!

In my case, I gave Kathi editorial privileges on our Indiegogo website. Her eagle eye caught little typo's and glitches that I never would have seen. She could make a living as a project exec. helper! Absolutely critical, in my opinion, for the success of a campaign!!

Don't blow this off. If you don't think you know anyone to do this, FIND someone. You can't wait until after you start the campaign. It will be too late!

As you go through the campaign, ask others *"What can I do to get the word out?"* While it is BEST to do that ***before*** the campaign, you must realize that you'll never get all the best ideas anyway so just keep working and asking and trying. And don't forget that NOBODY is going to work YOUR project as hard as YOU will work it. Not your best friend. Not your spouse. Not your Exec helper! *YOU **must set the pace. YOU must work the hardest. YOU must MAKE IT HAPPEN!!** You can do it too!*

CHAPTER 10 - THE END AND BEYOND

At some point, the campaign closes. Then what?

Thank everyone. Update everyone. Get your funds and deliver your perks. That's it, right?

WRONG!

You have a project to run! You have promises to keep! You have dreams to fulfill and you have people to help!

Get it done!

How you do your projects work is beyond the scope of this book. However here are a few things to keep in mind.

1. *If you do a good job you'll get no thanks.*
2. *If you do a great job you might get a smile.*
3. If you do a lousy job, the WORLD WILL KNOW!

This is both your project and it's PHASE 1 of Project #2. That's right! People who like what you do will likely donate again to your next project – IF you have a good track record on THIS project.

Maybe you are thinking, I won't ever do another project. And maybe you are right! But then again, maybe you are wrong. So let's err on the side of common sense and wise counsel. Let's do a GREAT job and let the next project come along when it does.

In the case of our project, as I type this, Kathi is printing return labels, getting the supplies ready and VERIFIYING the address of EVERY donor! (She's GREAT!) We don't even have our funds yet but we're ready when we get them.

Also, I've updated everyone on the list about where we now stand, what we've already done, what's next to do and I THANKED THEM AGAIN!

I want you to understand something that I believe in my heart is **CRITICAL...**

I am sincere when I thank these wonderful people. I am not just going through the motions. I am not just mouthing the words. I MEAN IT. I SINCERLEY MEAN IT! These people are the ones that said to me, *"YES! WE BELIEVE IN YOU! YES, WE WILL HELP YOU!"* **Friends, these are in the MAJORITY of the cases people I don't even KNOW! You BET I am thankful. You can count on the fact that I am going to thank them and sing their praises! They helped me make a dream of mine**

come true and we are going to help sick kids feel better, FASTER!! I'm on cloud nine!

As you work your project and as you enjoy the benefits that THEIR money provided to YOU, please thank them again. They deserve it. And I don't care if they donated $5.00 or $500.00, it ALL helps!

Going forward you are going to be in a position to do a lot of good. Are there people or other projects you could help with $5 or $10 or more? The more the merrier!!

<u>**If you EVER want to get help on another project, make certain this project goes GREAT!! Trust me – it IS that simple!**</u>

Good luck and may God richly bless you & your family!

ABOUT THE AUTHOR

Carl E. Jones, CFP ® is also known as Topper the Magic Clown to thousands of people all over North Texas and beyond. He and his wife, Marsha, a.k.a. Twinkle, are family entertainers who also are Therapeutic Clowns as well as maintaining a Children's ministry. They reside in Euless, Texas with their 4 Chihuahua's, 2 Macaw's and Snow White, their show-stealing chinchilla.

Carl, (Topper) has performed in 16 states and internationally to raise money and awareness for various children's hospitals since 1996. His comedy magic illusion and mind reading shows have raised over $54,000 for Shriner's and Scottish Rite Hospitals. He'd love to perform for you too!

His first crowd funding project sought $4,999 in 21 days. He raised the funds in 21 **_HOURS_** and went on to raise over $12,350 during the remaining 21 days of the campaign.

He's an exciting public speaker combining magic, jokes, gags and some other oddities to make every show different and FUN! He is available to speak to your group on a variety of issues and topics. *It won't be boring, you can count on that!* **Plus, he's a darn nice guy!**

Carl may be reached at
carl@carlejones.com
214-578-1601
Post Office Box 146
Euless, TX 76039

Please follow him on Facebook, Twitter,
LinkedIn & other Social Media outlets.

www.ingramcontent.com/pod-product-compliance
Lightning Source LLC
Chambersburg PA
CBHW071647170526
45166CB00003B/1472